My Name is Patrick

A Collection of Stories about People who Share my Name

By Allison Dearstyne

For my sparkplug, Patrick Vincent.

The name Patrick means "full of honor." Most people assume the name Patrick came from Ireland, but it came from the Latin word "Patricius." It wasn't a first name, but a title meaning "patrician," or nobly born. Your name was used in England and other places in Europe during the Middle Ages, but it didn't become popular in Ireland until the 1600's. That's because for hundreds of years most Irish people considered the name Patrick too sacred to use for their children. Today your name is most popular in Ireland!

Your name is over a thousand years old! Did you know that you share your name with some remarkable men? We will learn about these seven heroes named Patrick:

Saint Patrick
Patrick Mahomes
Patrick Pearse
Patrick Healy
Patrick Heron Watson
Patrick Ewing
Patrick Henry

Saint Patrick was the man who made your name famous! He wrote two autobiographies about his life, and this is what we know about him: He was born sometime around the year 400 in Roman Britain and was captured by Irish pirates when he was 16 years old. They took him to Ireland and made him a slave. For six bleak years he worked as a shepherd. This hardship led Patrick to depend on God. He recognized God's mercy and forgiveness through all his suffering.

While he was enslaved, Patrick remembered hearing a voice telling him he would soon go home, and his ship was ready. He escaped from his master and traveled far away to a port where there was a boat waiting. He convinced the captain to take him on board, and Patrick sailed back to Britain. Once he arrived on the shore, he wandered in the wilderness for over a month before he finally found his home. Patrick remained anchored in his faith in God and continued to study the Bible while living in Britain.

Would you believe that Patrick returned to Ireland by choice just a few years later? He was deeply moved by a vision he had while living as a free man in Britain. In his vision he saw a man from Ireland who gave him a letter from the Irish asking him to come back and walk among them.

So, Patrick returned as a Christian missionary to Ireland. As a foreigner, he was not protected by law, and he was the victim of several crimes during his time there. But Patrick considered all his hardships worthwhile.

He wrote this about the Irish: "Never before did they know of God except to serve idols and unclean things. But now they have become people of the Lord and are called children of Christ."

These are things that Patrick wrote about himself, and there are some legends about him too, which may or may not be true. One is that he used a three-leaf clover, or shamrock, to teach the Irish people about the Trinity. The Trinity is God the Father, the Son and the Holy Spirit, a teaching in the Christian faith. Of course, the shamrock is still a symbol for Saint Patrick's Day! There is another legend that Patrick banished all the snakes from Ireland, chasing them into the sea.

He is called the patron saint of Ireland, and we celebrate Saint Patrick's Day on March 17th in his honor. So, on Saint Patrick's Day this year, wear something green and think about selfless Saint Patrick!

Patrick Mahomes is the superstar quarterback for the Kansas City Chiefs. He was born in Texas in 1995 to an interracial couple. Patrick was always a natural athlete. In high school, he played football, baseball and basketball. Patrick said that playing different sports when he was younger helped him become a successful quarterback.

He played sports in college and entered the National Football League, or NFL draft at the end of his junior year. The Kansas City Chiefs chose Patrick in the first round of the draft in 2017. Football teams pick new players by draft, kind of like team captains picking other kids to be on their team in a schoolyard game. His second year playing, Patrick became the starting quarterback. Quarterbacks have a big job! They throw the football to players all over the field who run to get touchdowns.

For their first time in 50 years, the Chiefs made it to the Super Bowl in the 2019 season. The Chiefs won the game and Patrick was named Most Valuable Player. He was the youngest quarterback in NFL history to win that award! The Chiefs went to the Superbowl again in the 2020, 2022 and 2023 seasons and won twice. The Kansas City Chiefs are now considered a dynasty for all their wins. Patrick Mahomes is legendary!

His story doesn't end with being a superstar athlete. He says that his Christian faith is huge to him and whether he wins or loses, he wants to honor God. Patrick cares a lot about people! He created a charity called *15 and the Mahomies Foundation,* which improves the lives of children in need. Twice Patrick was named on *Time* 100's list of most influential people for all the good that he's done.

Patrick Mahomes is a champion! The next time your friends or family play football, join in and think about athletic Patrick Mahomes!

Patrick Pearse was an Irish patriot who fought for independence from Britain, even though it cost him everything. When he was born in Dublin in 1879, Britain ruled over Ireland. Inspired by family members who wanted independence, Patrick became a revolutionary when he was only ten. He promised that one day he would help win independence for Ireland.

His great-aunt taught him Gaelic, which is the Irish language. Patrick came to believe that Gaelic was an important piece in Ireland's identity as a nation. Gaelic was a dying language, and Patrick was afraid it would soon become extinct if Irish children didn't learn it in school. When Patrick grew up, his passion for the Irish language moved him to open a boy's school and a girl's school that taught both English and Gaelic.

He became known as an activist, which is someone who works to bring about political and social change. In 1912, some people in the English government suggested giving Ireland independence in an Irish Home Rule Bill. But the bill didn't pass as Patrick and other revolutionaries had hoped. As a result, Patrick secretly joined the Irish Republican Brotherhood, an organization committed to overthrowing British rule. He was chosen to be the president for this organization and called for a revolution against Britain in 1916.

At the beginning of this uprising, called the Easter Rising, Patrick stood outside the General Post Office in Dublin. There, he read the Proclamation of the Irish Republic, which is a document that he and some others had written declaring independence from England. To this day, the General Post Office is a symbol of Irish nationalism. After six days of fighting and heavy losses, he ordered the other revolutionaries to surrender.

Patrick Pearse died for his country after the Easter Rising, and he left behind a legacy of a being hero for the Irish nationalist cause. In 1922, Ireland finally gained independence. Always remember that freedom isn't free and remember the Irish patriot, Patrick Pearse!

Patrick Healy was the first American with Black ancestry to do many things: earn a doctorate, become a Jesuit priest, and become president of a mostly White university. He was born a slave in 1834 in Georgia. His mother was a slave, and his father was an Irish American. When he was born, Georgia state law did not allow his parents to marry, or Patrick and his siblings to attend school. So, Patrick's parents lovingly sent their children north, freeing them and providing for their education.

Eventually Patrick and his brothers attended college in Massachusetts, where they became Catholic. After Patrick graduated, he wanted to earn a doctorate, but he was discriminated against because of his race. So, he traveled to Belgium to earn a doctorate and was ordained to the priesthood. When he returned to the United States, Patrick taught philosophy at Georgetown University, where most of the students and all the other professors were White. After eight years, he moved up the ranks to become the school's president!

Patrick Healy is often called Georgetown University's second founder because he made so many big changes to the school. He modernized the small college and turned it into a major university. He added requirements for science, like chemistry and physics. Under his leadership, the schools of law and medicine were upgraded. A huge new building was constructed on campus that was later named in his honor. Patrick spent his later years traveling through the United States with his brother, serving the Catholic Church together as priests.

Throughout his life, education was important to Patrick Healy. When you are sitting in your classes at school, pay close attention and you can be like smart Patrick Healy!

Patrick Heron Watson was a Scottish surgeon who made enormous improvements in medical anesthesia. He was born in 1832 in Edinburgh. When Patrick grew up, he graduated from college and became a well-respected surgeon.

He had the gruesome job of operating on wounded soldiers during the Crimean War. Later, he spent 15 years teaching and operating on patients at Edinburgh University. In 1870, Patrick became one of the first professors to allow and encourage women to attend his classes in surgery. His opinion that women could be capable surgeons was unpopular since most people thought that women belonged only in the home. Patrick bravely defended his female students when most others would not.

He made operations safer and improved surgeries that included removing the thyroid, removing the knee joint, removing limbs and operating on the abdomen. He also discovered a new substance which was effective to use for anesthesia. Anesthesia is a temporary loss of feeling or awareness. It's an important part of any major surgery today because it makes the pain bearable for patients. Could you imagine if we had to undergo surgery without first feeling numb in the area where surgeons operated? It would be awful!

Later, Patrick helped found the Edinburgh Dental Hospital and encouraged his female students to join the staff. He received many honors including being elected President of the Royal College of Surgeons and knighted by King Edward VII. From then on, he became known as Sir Patrick Heron Watson.

If you haven't undergone surgery that requires anesthesia yet, you will! You have Sir Patrick Heron Watson to thank for a much better experience on the operating table!

Patrick Ewing is a basketball legend nicknamed "Warrior" and the "Hoya Destroya" for his tireless efforts and love for the game. He was born in Jamaica in 1962 and had a natural talent for soccer and cricket as a young boy. He moved to join his family in Massachusetts when he was 11 years old.

As a middle schooler he was already 6-foot-10! Someone introduced him to basketball, and he was awkward on the court at first. But in just a few years, he learned the game and was a star basketball player through high school. Patrick played basketball for Georgetown University and largely because of him, his team dominated. They made it to the National College Athletic Association, or the NCAA tournament three of his four years there. Patrick became a United States citizen while he was in college.

Then he was drafted to play basketball for the New York Knicks. Patrick was their best player too! He played for the Knicks for 15 years, and he was the only one on the team ever to play over 1,000 games! Patrick Ewing was named one of the Fifty Greatest Players in National Basketball Association, or NBA history.

Another highlight in his career was playing in the 1992 Olympics with the original "Dream Team" of the best basketball players in the United States. When he finished his career with the Knicks, his jersey number, 33, was retired. Retiring a player's number is an honor that means that no one else on a team can ever use that number.

You can see Patrick Ewing in the kid's movie *Space Jam*. The next time you shoot some hoops or dribble a basketball, think about athletic Patrick Ewing!

Patrick Henry was an American patriot whose biggest claim to fame was his powerful speeches. In 1736 Patrick was born in Virginia, the second of nine children. He was homeschooled growing up, and he loved to read and write. His hard work as a boy prepared him to be the capable public speaker that he later became!

When he grew up, it took Patrick many years and several professions before he became successful. As a young man he ran a store and tavern, but his business failed. He became a farmer, but his farmhouse burned to the ground. Learning from his failures and misfortune, Patrick decided to become a lawyer. He taught himself the skills he needed, and he was finally successful in his career.

As a lawyer, Patrick had an important role in making some changes to his Anglican state of Virginia, like allowing people to have freedom of religion. He felt that it was wrong for states to favor one religion over another. Freedom of religion would become a major principle not only for his state of Virginia, but for the United States.

When Patrick was born, Virginia was one of the 13 colonies in the Americas owned by Britain. Patrick was one of the first people to want independence. He made speeches about his beliefs and led people in a march against the policies made by Britain. Early on, some of the colonists said that Patrick's speeches were treasonous, or betrayal to his country. He didn't let other people stop him though! Patrick helped to unite the colonists to begin a revolution.

He said, "The distinctions between Virginians, Pennsylvanians, New Yorkers and New Englanders, are no more. I am not a Virginian, but an American." One year later he gave a speech to a group of colonists who were arguing over what to do about their problems with Britain: Should they solve the problems peacefully or begin a revolution?

In his most powerful speech, Patrick Henry exclaimed, "Give me liberty or give me death!" The American Revolution began shortly after.

A few years into the war, there was a long and hard winter for the Americans. It looked like the British would win the war. Patrick became sick, but helped the American troops by sending food and defending his friend George Washington when many others criticized him.

George Washington later said of Patrick Henry, "I have always respected and esteemed him."

After the Americans won the Revolutionary War, they struggled under a weak government. After a few years, a stronger government was created to fix the problems of the old one. Patrick did not support the new government until the Bill of Rights was added to it. The Bill of Rights guaranteed American citizens rights, like freedom of speech and religion. Patrick worked for the Bill of Rights to be passed and it remains part of the United States Constitution to this day.

Because of his special role in the early history of the United States, we call Patrick Henry a founding father. He has been called "the boldest of patriots," "the Trumpet," and "the Voice" of the American Revolution. The next time you see an American flag, give it a salute and think about founding father Patrick Henry!

This page is all about you!

_____ was born on

_____

As a baby, Patrick _____

_____

As a little boy, Patrick _____

_____

Patrick is especially good at _____

_____

Patrick is often described as _____

_____

Patrick makes people laugh when he _____

_____

One day Patrick would like to _____

_____

This page is for making a self-portrait. A self-portrait is a picture of you, drawn by you!

Bibliography

Encyclopaedia Britannica Editors. "Patrick Pearse." *Encyclopaedia Britannica.* Encyclopaedia Britannica, inc. 01 May. 2018. Web. 12 Jul. 2018.

Espiritu, Allison. "Patrick Healy (1834-1910)." *blackpast.org.* Blackpast. 03 Mar. 2007. Web. 29 Sep. 2019.

NBA.com Staff. "Legends Profile: Patrick Ewing." *2018 NBA Media Ventures, LLC.* Web. 12 Jul. 2018.

O'Raifeartaigh, Tarlach. "St. Patrick." *Encyclopaedia Britannica.* Encyclopaedia Britannica, inc. 23 Apr. 2018. Web. 12 Jul. 2018.

Wikipedia contributors. "Patrick (given name)." *Wikipedia, The Free Encyclopedia.* Wikipedia, The Free Encyclopedia, 22 Jun. 2018. Web. 12 Jul. 2018.

Wikipedia contributors. "Patrick Ewing." *Wikipedia, The Free Encyclopedia.* Wikipedia, The Free Encyclopedia, 5 Jul. 2018. Web. 12 Jul. 2018.

Wikipedia contributors. "Patrick Francis Healy." *Wikipedia, The Free Encyclopedia.* Wikipedia, The Free Encyclopedia, 24 Sep. 2019. Web. 26 Sep. 2019.

Wikipedia contributors. "Patrick Henry." *Wikipedia, The Free Encyclopedia.* Wikipedia, The Free Encyclopedia, 7 May. 2018. Web. 12 Jul. 2018.

Wikipedia contributors. "Patrick Mahomes." *Wikipedia, The Free Encyclopedia*. Wikipedia, The Free Encyclopedia, 23 Feb. 2024. Web. 26 Feb. 2024.

Wikipedia contributors. "Patrick Pearse." *Wikipedia, The Free Encyclopedia*. Wikipedia, The Free Encyclopedia, 6 Jul. 2018. Web. 12 Jul. 2018.

Wikipedia contributors. "Patrick Heron Watson." *Wikipedia, The Free Encyclopedia*. Wikipedia, The Free Encyclopedia, 30 Mar. 2019. Web. 26 Aug. 2019.

Wikipedia contributors. "Saint Patrick." *Wikipedia, The Free Encyclopedia*. Wikipedia, The Free Encyclopedia, 23 Jun. 2018. Web. 12 Jul. 2018.

www.ingramcontent.com/pod-product-compliance
Lightning Source LLC
Chambersburg PA
CBHW042111040426
42448CB00002B/227

* 9 7 8 1 9 4 8 6 5 9 0 3 1 *